THE LAND OF

STREAM AND TOR

By William Crossing

(With an Introduction by Brian Le Messurier)

FOREST PUBLISHING

First published in 1994 by FOREST PUBLISHING, Woodstock, Liverton, Newton Abbot, Devon TQ12 6JJ

British Library Cataloguing in Publication Data

A catalogue record for this book is available from the British Library.

ISBN 0–9515274–5–2

Forest Publishing

Editorial, design and layout, and colour photography by:
Mike Lang

Typeset by:
Carnaby Typesetting, Torquay, Devon TQ1 1EG

Printed and bound in Great Britain by:
The Latimer Trend Group, Plymouth, Devon PL6 7PL

Cover photographs:

Front – The River Lyd below Bra Tor (Brattor)

Back – The Wallabrook Clapper Bridge, Scorhill Down

CONTENTS

ACKNOWLEDGEMENTS

The Publishers wish to sincerely thank all of those people who have provided assistance during the compilation of this book.
Particular thanks are due to Mr. Ian Maxted of the Devon County Council Library Headquarters in Exeter; to Mr. Colin Davison, editor of *The Western Morning News*; to Mr. Brian Le Messurier for writing the Introduction; to Miss Elisabeth Stanbrook for kindly providing most of the photographs which add so much to this book.

LIST OF ILLUSTRATIONS

INTRODUCTION

This little book was written by the 44-year-old William Crossing when he had reached a turning-point in his life. His health had begun to deteriorate, and he was no longer able to be out in all weathers, so he used the opportunity of being at home to write this extended essay about Dartmoor which was one of his first ventures into quasi-journalism. But who was this man, and why should we want to read this book 102 years after it was first published?

William Crossing was born in Plymouth on 14 November 1847 and spent much of his boyhood in that city. As a child he was encouraged by his mother to interest himself in the antiquities and traditions of the countryside, and since the family spent holidays in a cottage on Roborough Down he was introduced to Dartmoor at an early age.

When he left school he was apprenticed to a sail-cloth manufacturer, but, disliking the trade, ran away to sea and sailed to Canada. By the time he was twenty he had returned to Plymouth and was working for his father. In his spare time he wrote poetry and plays, and also took every opportunity to visit the moor which remained his chief interest.

Mr Crossing senior, no doubt feeling that a position of responsibility would benefit his son, sent William to supervise the family mill at South Brent. But away from parental control William indulged in his twin delights of drama and Dartmoor more freely than ever; he ran a local theatre, which after an initial success failed financially, and the moor was at his doorstep.

Theatricals continued to attract, and so William formed his own professional drama group with which he went on tour. When this venture failed, too, he returned to the South Brent mill, which his long-suffering father had kept going, and resumed his Dartmoor explorations. Perhaps because of his lack of interest it was not long before the canvas mill closed down, and he was left struggling for his livelihood. It is worth remembering, however, that with the development of steam propulsion at sea the need for ships' sails would have diminished.

He had married in 1872 and shortly afterwards began to keep careful records of his Dartmoor excursions and studies. With no desire to return to business he determined to earn his daily bread by writing, but he and his wife, Emma, stayed on at South Brent until the 1890s, when they moved to Brent Tor, and then to Mary Tavy. Until his health began to decline, Crossing had constantly walked or ridden the moor, never shirking a soaking in his tweed clothes and leather gaiters. Wherever he went he made friends with the moormen, and he was a popular figure in the group round the peat fire in the evenings, when he would play tunes on his tin whistle, or recite an improvised rhyme describing his wanderings of the day.

Crossing had joined the Dartmoor Preservation Association soon after it was formed in 1883, and was a member of the Devonshire Association from 1881 to 1891, although he never contributed to the *Transactions* of that body. From being a person of some substance – he writes in *Amid Devonia's Alps* of having 'a man' called George in 1872 – he became so impoverished that he had to resign from both Associations.

Much of Crossing's writing up to the early 1890s had been for a journal called *The Western Antiquary* which ran from 1881 to 1895. A glance at pages 144 and 145 of *The Dartmoor Bibliography* (compiled by Peter Hamilton-Leggett, Devon Books, 1992) shows a lengthy list of his notes and queries printed in this learned periodical, together with the long-running series of articles called 'Crockern Tor, and the Ancient Stannary Parliament' which the journal published over several years. Contributors to *The Western Antiquary* were not paid. Up to this time only *Amid Devonia's Alps* of Crossing's books had not first had an airing in the pages of *The Western Antiquary.*

In 1891 he wrote a long article 'The Land of Stream and Tor' for *Doidge's Western Counties Illustrated Annual for 1892.* (This curious publication came out each year about Christmas time) One feels it was prepared with a view to separate and simultaneous publication as a small book about Dartmoor for it appeared under its own covers as *The Land of Stream and Tor* at about the same time, and it has become one of Crossing's scarcest books on the secondhand market. To understand the circumstances better it is as well to know what *Doidge's Almanac,* as it was often called, consisted of.

It was founded by Thomas Sweet Doidge (1833–1889), the leading Plymouth stationer and bookseller, in 1869, as *The West of England Illustrated*, but soon changed its name. The contents were a surprising miscellany of gardening hints, jokes and anecdotes, recipes, a list of carriers, tide-tables, the phases of the moon, a list of magistrates, poems, etc., etc. After a few years, short stories appeared. The founder was a religious man, so the early editions contain advice of an 'improving nature'. The advertisements for novelties, foundation garments, cabin trunks and a host of other long-discarded objects evoke the late nineteenth century as few other publications can. *Doidge's Almanac* struggled on until 1954, being published for the last thirteen years by *The Western Morning News.* Prose contributors to these pages are unlikely to have been paid, or paid much – most of the writers were aspiring authors anxious to get a foot in the literary door – but Crossing felt that his piece would get a general circulation in the almanac, while the off-print would appeal to the Dartmoor devotee, and regardless of the lack of financial recompense in the pages of the almanac, as a separate publication it would provide a monetary return.

One puzzling aspect of *The Land of Stream and Tor* must be mentioned. On the title page the author is given as 'William Crossing, F.S.L.' None of Crossing's other books bear this qualification, and it is not mentioned in any of his obituary notices or subsequent accounts of his life. The present writer has attempted to discover what these letters might mean, and has contacted the Royal Society of Literature of the

William Crossing as he was in about 1895. The drawing is a copy of a photograph in *West-Country Poets*, 1896, and first appeared in *The Western Morning News* in 1904.

United Kingdom who say that the letters F.R.S.L. have been in use since 1823. Present-day lists of abbreviations in the Exeter reference library are no help, and I have drawn a blank with the Society of Authors and various national linguistic and library institutions. I am tempted to think that Crossing was playing a practical joke, but if anyone reading this can put forward a likely suggestion I would be pleased to hear it, and the editor of the *Dartmoor Magazine* may consider its publication!

Crossing did not write in *Doidge's Almanac* again, but became editor of *The Westcountry Annual*, which was less concerned with tables of information but was more literary in content. He also brought out a small book called *Cricket Averages* and other unexpected titles like *Mount Edgecumbe Souvenir*, *The Book of Fair Devon* and *The Marine and River Guide to the South Coast of Devon and Cornwall.*

With the end of the nineteenth century Crossing saw his opportunity to write a series of articles telling the story of the hundred years just past in so far as they affected Dartmoor. Thus 'A Hundred Years on Dartmoor' began its seventeen-week run in *The Western Morning News* in June 1900. These articles were published a year later in book form with the addition of photographs and several appendices. (It is a matter of interest that the book carried the words *One Hundred Years* ... on the cover, but *A Hundred Years* ... on the title page) The book was highly successful and went into five editions.

Thus it was as a result of the success of *A Hundred Years* ... that Crossing was engaged to write 'Echoes of an Ancient Forest'. On the 29 October 1901 *The Western Morning News* printed the following paragraphs:

Echoes of an Ancient Forest

> We have pleasure in announcing that we shall in a few days begin the publication of a further series of articles, under the above title, by Mr William Crossing, whose *One Hundred Years on Dartmoor* has proved so popular both in serial and in book form.
>
> The series about to begin will trace the various waymarks in Dartmoor history from the time of King John down to the close of the eighteenth century, at which point the volume now in its third edition takes up the story.

The first weekly article followed on the 1 November 1901.

Reading between the lines, one suspects that 'Echoes ...' was commissioned by *The Western Morning News* with a view to later publication as a book, but this never happened – until now, for *Echoes of an Ancient Forest* is being issued concurrently by Forest Publishing, also with a scene-setting introduction.

Numerous other articles by Crossing followed, in a variety of West Country newspapers, and *The Dartmoor Bibliography* shows his incredible output at this time. In 1906 he became tutor to the three sons of Mr W. P. Collins, and teaching was carried on alongside work on his magnum opus, the *Guide to Dartmoor*. This went into three editions, and has been reprinted in recent years.

Crossing's last years are touched with sadness. Mr Collins arranged a public subscription for him on his 70th birthday, but shortly afterwards the old couple had to move to Ivybridge, where relations lived, for Mrs Crossing was ailing. When constant nursing became necessary she was admitted to Tavistock Institution (the workhouse in common parlance), and she died there on 6 June 1921.

Mr Collins found accommodation for his old friend at Mary Tavy, and Crossing lived there for a while. In 1924, while he was away from home, the woman who looked after his rooms found a mass of papers and, because mice had damaged them, burnt the lot. Since Crossing had been preparing a history of Dartmoor, and the notes represented a lifetime's work, the loss was irreplaceable. For twelve weeks from 9 July 1925 he was a patient at Tavistock Institution, but in October he was taken to Cross Park Nursing Home, in Plymouth, where he spent his last three years. During this time Mr Collins paid the bills, which amounted to several hundred pounds. While at Cross Park he published his last book, a volume of poems called *Cranmere*, after the principal work it contained. His first book, *Leaves from*

Sherwood (1868) was also poetry.

William Crossing died on 3 September 1928, and is buried with his wife in Mary Tavy churchyard. The grave is north-east of the church, and standing by it one can see the western slopes of Dartmoor swelling up less than a mile away.

Our debt to Crossing is enormous. He was the pioneer of a rational study of Dartmoor. He discovered stone crosses whose whereabouts had long been forgotten, and recorded their position in his books on the subject. He was the accurate chronicler of customs now gone from the country calendar, and his collection of folklore tales was made before the memory of them was lost forever. He gained the confidence and respect of Dartmoor people and from them learned the obscure place-names, and as a result of frequent forays across the whole of the moor at all times of the year acquired a minute knowledge of every hill and valley, and many of the antiquities which had been the subject of unproven theorising. He can be relied upon to present the true Dartmoor, unadorned by flights of fancy. It is good that a wider public can read his words once more, for although written so long ago, they have stood the test of time.

Brian Le Messurier
August 1994

*****

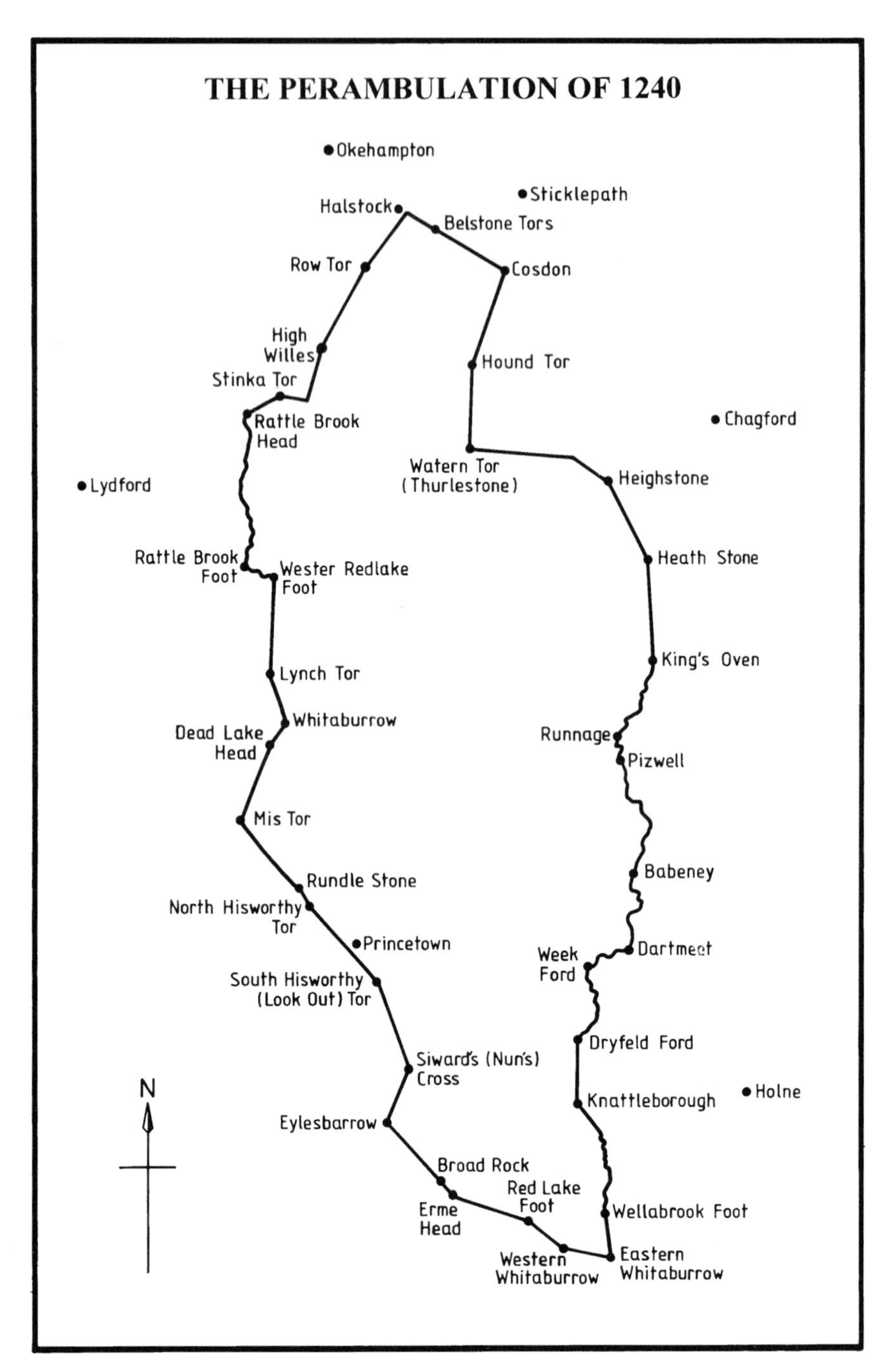
THE PERAMBULATION OF 1240
Okehampton
Sticklepath
Halstock
Belstone Tors
Row Tor
Cosdon
High
Willes
Hound Tor
Stinka Tor
Rattle Brook
Head
Chagford
Watern Tor
(Thurlestone)
Heighstone
Lydford
Rattle Brook
Foot
Wester Redlake
Foot
Heath Stone
Lynch Tor
King's Oven
Whitaburrow
Dead Lake
Head
Runnage
Pizwell
Mis Tor
Babeney
Rundle Stone
North Hisworthy
Tor
Princetown
Week
Ford
Dartmeet
South Hisworthy
(Look Out) Tor
Dryfeld Ford
Siward's (Nun's)
Cross
N
Knattleborough
Holne
Eylesbarrow
Broad Rock
Red Lake
Foot
Erme
Head
Wellabrook Foot
Western
Whitaburrow
Eastern
Whitaburrow

THE LAND OF

STREAM AND TOR.

BY

WILLIAM CROSSING, F.S.L.

RE-PRINTED (BY PERMISSION) FROM

Doidge's Western Counties Illustrated Annual for 1892.

For Private Circulation only.

PLYMOUTH:
DOIDGE & CO., 169 AND 170, UNION STREET

1891

The Land of Stream and Tor.

IN the fairest county of England, for so has Devonshire been with justice styled, surrounded by land smiling under the hand of cultivation, is situated the wild stretch of hill-country known as Dartmoor. Although wholly within the southern portion, yet there are few elevated spots in the county, or in East Cornwall, from which it is not visible, while its loftier eminences may be seen from parts of Somerset and Dorset.

If we take a map of Devon and examine it we shall notice that the northern point of Dartmoor is at Okehampton, and the southern just above Ivybridge, and measuring this distance carefully we shall find it to be rather over twenty-three miles. In this measurement is included the enclosed tract of land on the north, known as Okehampton Park, and which may fairly be reckoned as being a portion of the moor. The breadth of Dartmoor will be found to vary from about nine miles to seventeen, but we may consider the average to be somewhat under twelve miles. These distances, however, are what the map shows us, but the pedestrian who essays to cover the length or breadth of Dartmoor must expect to find his walk considerably longer, owing to the conformation of the country, which consists of swelling hills, and where the rivers leave their upland birth-place for the meads below, deep valleys, with steep and rugged sides.

Until within the last few years this district was to the tourist, and even to many of those who dwelt around it, a sealed book, but facilities having of late been offered for visiting it, its attractions are becoming more widely known, and require nothing further to be rightly appreciated. An interest has been created in Dartmoor, which those who have known it long and loved it well do not wonder at, for even a slight knowledge of it is sufficient to awaken such, and as that knowledge is extended so the interest will expand. All true men of Devon must feel proud of Dartmoor, for it is one of the very few spots in our island where the eye may behold Nature in her wilder form, and in its more remote parts rest upon a broad expanse where man has not intruded his handiwork.

There is something particularly soothing in being able to leave the "madding crowd's ignoble strife," and betake oneself to Dartmoor, where old world customs still obtain. Here the weary wanderer may find a restful land, a land of babbling brooks, a land of freedom, where grows the heather and the broom, and the golden furze. A land where his ramblings amid the hills will bring him face to face with vestiges of the rude erections of a people long passed away, or where he may, directing his steps into its inmost recesses, look around and see nought but what God himself has made. And if he seeks this wide moor to find renewed health, what grateful draughts of pure air may he not drink in, and how elastic will his spirits be as he treads the purple heather and climbs the lofty hill, crested by the rocky tor. Or if with canvas and colours he visits it to limn its varied scenes, what charming "bits" are constantly presented to his view. Should the geologist, with hammer in hand, determine upon investigating its clatters and its tors, what a vast field lies before him ; and if the antiquary should roam over its steeps in quest of objects belonging to a by-gone age, how much is there to delight him and to repay him for his search. It has been said that to Dartmoor must be awarded the blue ribbon among districts where pre-historic antiquities are found, and this will be readily allowed when the careful investigator discovers what a number of interesting examples there exist. Cairns, kistvaens, stone circles, menhirs, and stone-rows are numerous, while hut circles, some of them being remarkably fine examples, are to be seen on every part of the moor. Many large enclosures, or pounds, are also to be met with, the ruined walls being composed of blocks of granite, in some instances of exceedingly large size. Curious clapper bridges span the streams, and are particularly interesting They are formed of huge slabs, laid from abutment to pier, several feet above the river bed, and offered a means of crossing to pack-horses when the rivers, swollen by rains, were too deep to be forded. Vestiges of early mining abound on all the river banks, and together with what has been gained by historical research, do much to throw a light upon the doings of the tinners of the moor. The sportsman, too, has reason to be glad of the existence of such a place as Dartmoor, for many a rapid gallop does the hunter take over its breezy heights in pursuit of Reynard. And bold riding does it require and right good English pluck does it call forth ; while if he seek sport of a softer sort the numerous clear streams that rise among its hills abound in trout, and the "contemplative man" strolling along their banks with his rod, if he be a deft hand at his work, will often be rewarded with a well-filled creel. Nor must we forget how much Devon itself owes to Dartmoor. The streams that flow from this "liberal mountain urn" lend to it its greatest charm, and are truly the source of its fatness. The desolate upland with its rock-strewn slopes, and its grim tors often shrouded in mist, is the bounteous mother of the smiling fields and waving woods that lie around it, and which have earned for Devonia the title of the land of flowers.

Of the early history of Dartmoor we know little beyond what we are able to gather from an examination of its rude stone remains, and these show us that a primitive people once dwelt among its hills. They consist of vestiges of the habitations of the living, and the sepulchral monuments of the dead. The first, which take the form of ruined basements of dwellings, circular in shape, and varying in diameter from about eighteen to twenty-four feet,* and which are known as hut circles, are generally found in clusters, termed not very happily, villages. These are sometimes encircled with a wall, now always seen in ruins, the space enclosed being occasionally as much as four acres in extent, or even more. This wall appears to have been raised to a height of several feet, probably six or eight, the faces being of stone, and having the space between them filled with turf, and on the top of this it is not unlikely that more turf was piled, in order to give it a greater elevation, and it would seem to have usually been about eight or ten feet in width. Within the enclosure formed by this strong rampart the flocks and herds of the settlers were probably driven at night in order to ensure their protection from wolves. Many of the dwellings were placed on the outside of the enclosure, so that it seems likely that those within it were occupied by such as had charge of, or who owned, the cattle which it sheltered. It is also, of course, possible that the wall was designed to afford protection, in case such were needed, to the inhabitants of the settlement; but if so, such must have been but a secondary consideration, or we should scarcely have found, as we do, so many of the dwelling places on the outside of it. Nor, if such protection for the dwellers were necessary, is it easy to understand why we find large groups of these hut circles without any enclosing wall at all. On the moor these enclosures are called pounds, and are always looked upon as having been designed for the purpose we have indicated, that of penning cattle, and that they were forts or camps as some have imagined the evidence which an examination of them affords, does not seem to show.

Grimspound is a well-known example of these enclosures, its wall being very striking in consequence of its great width, and of the size of the blocks of granite which compose it. It is situated on the eastern side of the moor, near the northern extremity of Hameldon, a

* Exceptional examples are found that are not more than ten feet in diameter, and in the opposite extreme some few are as much as thirty feet.

lofty and conspicuous ridge, forming a barrier between the wide wastes and the pleasant vale of Widecombe. Another remarkably fine enclosed group is situated on the Brockhill stream, a tributary of the Avon, which rises in south Dartmoor and flowing by Brent, Loddiswell, and Aveton Gifford, pours its waters into the sea at Bantham, near the rock known as Borough Island.

Not far below this group, on the same river, is another, known as The Rings, which is not only the largest on the moor, but is also the most curious as possessing a number of small courts or pens within it. The enclosing wall has a circuit of nine hundred and seventy-five yards, or considerably over half-a-mile, and was originally about ten feet wide, as is shown in many places where the stones are laid in courses. On the Erme river, on a slope of a hill called Brown Heath, are other fine enclosures, which, from their proximity to an ancient drift-pound, have taken its name, and are now known as Erme Pound Rings. On the Yealm, and not a very great distance above the well-known wooded vale of Hawns and Dendles, there are also enclosures containing hut circles, and a great many others in different parts of the moor might be mentioned. Of the unenclosed groups the better known are those under Great Mis Tor, on the western side of Dartmoor, and in the vicinity of Kes Tor, above Chagford, on the eastern; but important clusters occur in other parts of the moor, in fact, there is no portion of it, with the exception of the central morasses of its northern and southern divisions, where the pedestrian in the course of a ramble of any extent would not meet with them.

Of the remains which constituted memorials of the departed we may enumerate the cairn, and the barrow, the dolmen or cromlech, the kistvaen, the circle of upright stones, and the single upright stone, or menhir. The cairn, which consists of a great heap of stones piled over the dead, is found much more frequently upon Dartmoor than the barrow, which served the same purpose, but is composed of earth. This is, of course, just what we should expect to find in a district where stone is not only abundant, but where it was to be procured in sufficient quantity without any greater labour than that of collecting the fragments that so plentifully cover so many of the hill-sides. Researches among cairns and barrows in many parts of the kingdom and elsewhere, have revealed to us the fact that the interments in or beneath them were made in a variety of ways. Sometimes the body was placed in a kist, or coffin formed of slabs; at others it was simply laid on the ground and covered with the stones of the cairn, while not infrequently it was first burnt and the ashes deposited in an urn of earthenware, over which the mound was then piled. Occasionally there have been found with these cinerary urns flint implements and ancient weapons, also drinking cups and various kinds of ornaments. The cairns and barrows of Dartmoor have mostly been opened, but some still exist which have not yet undergone any examination. Of the contents of those which were rifled before our time we unfortunately know nothing, no record having been kept, and the researches conducted in recent times have, unfortunately,

A clapper bridge, near Teign Head Farm

Grimspound

Spinsters' Rock

Dunnabridge Pound – 'the quoit now forms a canopy over a stone seat'

One of the numerous kistvaens on Dartmoor

Stall Moor Circle

Baredown Man and Devil's Tor

Western Whitaburrow

Nun's, or Siward's, Cross

Bennett's Cross, near
the Warren House Inn

yielded but little. In the year 1872, the late Mr. Spence Bate opened one under Pen Beacon, the fine hill overlooking the village of Cornwood, or, as it is locally called, Cross. Within it was an imperfect kist, and in the peat forming the bottom of this he found an implement of soft slate. It was oval in shape, and about three and a-half-inches long, and an inch wide, very thin, and having the ends bevelled. Mr. Bate imagined it to have been employed in the fashioning of clay vessels. Beyond numerous fragments of pottery found in different parts of the cairn he discovered nothing else; but in an examination of a barrow on Hameldon he was much more fortunate. Here he met with a mass of comminuted bones mixed with earth, the blade of a bronze dagger, and an ornament of amber, studded with gold pins, which it has been conjectured may have formed the pommel of this weapon, or possibly, as it was considered too large for that purpose, that of a sword. A careful examination, extending over three days, of the westernly cairn on Three Barrows, an eminence rising above the eastern bank of the Erme, some four-and-a-half or five miles above Ivybridge, was unattended by any result; the more to be wondered at, as from the size of these cairns an important interment would naturally be looked for within them. The very last time that Mr. Bate was on Dartmoor, some three weeks before his death, the writer assisted him at the opening of a cairn on another part of the moor, but nothing was discovered. Mr. S. H. Slade, in 1878, opened a small cairn, near Thornworthy, in the neighbourhood of Chagford, which was found to contain two kists, in one of which was an implement of flint, and in the other two more tools of the same and a portion of an urn. One of these kists was *afterwards removed* to the museum of the Torquay Natural History Society. Let us hope that Dartmoor may be saved from very many such *aids* to the preservation of its antiquities! Flint chips, rude knives or arrow-heads, are found in all parts of the moor. They have been dug up near the Princetown Prisons, and have also been discovered lying on the surface of the ground in some parts. Not very long since in some fields close to the borders of the moor, on its eastern side, an exceedingly large number were found; and if we except the more central portions of Dartmoor before referred to, there are probably few parts of it on which these relics might not be obtained.

The dolmen, or cromlech, is not of common occurrence on the moor, and there cannot be said to exist more than one complete specimen upon it. But at Drewsteignton, which is not very far removed from the borders, is a very perfect example, well-known to tourists as the Spinsters' Rock. The dolmen seems to have been nothing more than a huge kistvaen, its size being not improbably due to its having enclosed the remains of someone of importance. From their having frequently been discovered in various parts within a cairn it has been suggested that originally they were all buried beneath such, and have from various causes been denuded of their covering of stones or earth. They consist of one huge stone, sometimes of an enormous weight, supported at a height of several feet above the ground upon others, generally three in number, although examples are not wanting where the supporters are more. They occur in different parts of the world, and are the most striking of all the old stone monuments. The one that remains on Dartmoor is situated at Dunnabridge, immediately within the entrance to the drift-pound there; and the quoit now forms a canopy over a stone seat. It would appear to have been a dolmen of similar character to Kits Cotty House, in Kent. A curiously supported rock on a tor on the common to the east of the village of Shaugh has been by some considered to be a dolmen, but it lacks the true characteristics of the cromlech, the supposed quoit, or capstone, being supported partly by a natural rock. There are, however, not wanting examples of undoubted dolmens on Dartmoor, but unfortunately they no longer maintain their erect position.

The kistvaen is a small sarcophagus formed of slabs. The name, which is composed of two Celtic words, signifies a stone chest, and such in reality the kistvaen is. Two stones were placed so as to form the sides, while two others constituted the ends. These were sunk in the ground and covered with another flat stone, the whole probably having a mound heaped over it, as in the manner it has been suggested the dolmens were covered, and this was not infrequently enclosed within a small circle of upright stones. The kist, of course, varied in size, but was generally from two to three feet in width, and from four to five feet long, or even more, and of a depth of about three feet. When the body was not burnt and the ashes merely deposited in the kist, it was often placed in such a posture that the chin nearly touched the knees, and was sometimes laid upon its side. Kistvaens are exceedingly numerous on Dartmoor, and the wanderer may often chance upon one of these pre-historic graves as he passes over its wastes.

The stone circle is also not rare on the moor. This is sometimes seen enclosing a kistvaen as already remarked, and is also found without any such object within it, but that it marked a burial-place the evidence which we possess leaves us no room to doubt. Some of the circles on the moor have long rows of stones extending from them, but with what object is not at first very clear. These rows are sometimes double, the two lines being about four-and-a-half feet from each other, and these have been termed stone avenues. Various suggestions have been made as to their purpose. Mr. Fergusson, whose opinion is entitled to great respect, considered it likely that these lines of stones were set up by some victorious tribe to commemorate a battle; the rows representing the contending armies, or two lines of the conquering one. As it is known that some savage nations set up rows of sticks with a similar object, the suggestion must certainly be admitted to have some weight. But some of these stone rows on Dartmoor are only single lines, and from the distance they extend, one of them being nearly two miles in length, seem to preclude the idea of their having been formed for such a purpose. Many tumuli have elsewhere been found to possess a covered passage to the interior.

That this passage should be extended by means of upright stones leading directly to the opening in the cairn it does not seem unreasonable to suppose would in time be the case ; at all events we know that rows of stones were set up to form ways to some of the most important of the columnar circles, as at Abury in Wiltshire, akin to which are the even more celebrated avenues of Carnac, in Brittany. The stone-rows of Dartmoor if carefully examined with a due regard to the remains with which they are connected, will be found to be much of the same character, though, of course, on a very different scale; and that they are to be regarded as a portion of the monument they lead to, there seems to be no valid reason to doubt. The row just referred to as extending for nearly two miles over the moor, has a dilapidated kistvaen at one extremity of it, and a fine stone circle at the other.

The menhir, or single upright stone, is generally found in connection with other remains of a sepulchral character. There are some good examples on Dartmoor, several of them still standing erect. On Long Ash Hill, above Merivale Bridge, and close to the well-known avenues, there is one. Another, nearly eleven feet high, stands in a lonely situation near Devil's Tor, and goes by the name of Baredown Man.* In the neighbourhood of Kes Tor is another, called the Longstone, and there is one by the same name on Dean Moor.

These megalithic remains have by some been termed Druidical, and supposed to be the work of that mysterious priesthood. The older antiquaries greatly favoured this idea, but modern research has shown that there is not the slightest evidence to connect the two ; and cairn and barrow, dolmen and kistvaen, stone circle and menhir, can only be regarded as memorials of the dead. From the very earliest ages of the world men have chosen by such erections to keep alive the memory of those who had passed away. In Genesis xxxv. 20, we read that Jacob set up a pillar upon the grave of Rachel, and in the second book of Samuel, xviii. 18, it is recorded that Absalom erected a similar monument, "for he said, I have no son to keep my name in remembrance : and he called the pillar after his own name : and it is called unto this day Absalom's place." Herodotus and Plutarch and other ancient authors refer to the practice of raising mounds over the dead, and in an Anglo-Saxon poem, which is fortunately preserved, there is given a description of the burning of the dead body of a chieftain named Beowulf, and of the placing of certain articles beside the remains and the heaping over it of the mound.

A desire will naturally follow the contemplation of the rude monuments of early times which we find upon Dartmoor to learn something, if it be possible, of the people who erected them, and what it was that prompted them to settle among these wild hills. While it is obviously not easy to satisfy ourselves as to the first part of this enquiry, an answer to the second is forthcoming. It will be noticed by the careful investigator that the hut settlements of the moor are all of them in close proximity to old tin stream-works, and that

* A corruption of *maen*, the Celtic word for *stone*.

where these latter are most extensive there the more important of the groups of hut circles are to be found. Tin was exported from the western parts of Britain centuries before the birth of Christ, the Cassiterides, by which name the peninsula now comprehended by the counties of Devon and Cornwall, or a portion of them, is supposed to be indicated, being mentioned by the Greek historian Herodotus, as the place whence that metal was obtained. It is also believed that there were even earlier traders in the tin of Britain, the Phœnicians having being thought by some to have visited our shores for the purpose of obtaining it, and such is, of course, not improbable. Herodotus wrote about four centuries and a half before the Christian era, but being unacquainted with the Cassiterides he furnishes us with no particulars regarding them. We, however, get some information about the tin mining of the southern parts of our island from Diodorus, who wrote about forty years B.C., some four centuries later than Herodotus, and the subject of metals being found in Britain is also mentioned by other early writers. With such evidence before us we can have no difficulty in believing that the chief object that the settlers of those distant days had in seeking the uplands of Devon was the procuring of tin, but it would at the same time be rash to assume that all the remains date back to so early a period. Many were probably erected several centuries after the Christian era, while numbers of the hut circles no doubt belong to a very much more modern time. Nor must it be forgotten that the stream-works do not all of them now discover to us the remains of the mining of the earliest tinners, for in mediæval times Dartmoor was the scene of numberless operations in this direction, and there is little doubt that these later tinners, in addition to forming new workings, searched for the metal on and near the older ones.

The ancient inhabitants of Devon and Cornwall were the Danmonii, a tribe of Celts who have left traces of their occupation, as in fact they have done all over Europe in many of the place-names, not a few of the rivers and hills of the moor bearing Celtic appellations. We know, too, that the Saxon in later times settled upon it, for no small portion of the nomenclature of Dartmoor is in that tongue; and there have also been those who have contended for a Scandinavian occupation of the moor. The British kingdom of Danmonium held out for long against the Saxons, but in the year 926 Athelstan drove out the Britons from Exeter to beyond the Tamar. Half-a-century later the Danes re-appeared on the coasts, and afterwards in 997 ascended the Tavy and burnt Tavistock Abbey, carrying their ravages as far as Lydford, which at that period was one of the principal towns in Devon.

In Domesday we find no mention whatever of Dartmoor, but as that great survey of the Norman Conqueror took notice only of such lands as would yield a revenue, an uncultivated district such as the moor, it has been pointed out, would not be likely to be included. Lydford is mentioned, and in that parish a very large portion of Dartmoor lies, but the Domesday entry refers not to this, but only to the borough.

The first mention which we have of Dartmoor by name is in a charter of King John, given in the fifth year of his reign, A.D. 1204. Previous to this time all Devon, it would seem, had been under the harsh forest laws, and by the charter in question it was sought to release it from the operation of those cruel edicts, or, in other words, to disafforest it, with the exception of Dartmoor and Exmoor, the bounds of which, it appears from the document, had been set out in the reign of Henry I. At about the same time that the barons obtained from King John that glorious foundation of our liberty—Magna Charta—he had been compelled also to grant a charter of forests, by which all lands, unless it were Royal demesne, that had been afforested since the reign of the first Henry, were ordered to be disafforested. It had been found necessary to demand such a charter for the redress of the grievances from which the people had suffered in consequence of the number of forests formed by the Norman kings, with whom the gratification of their passion for the chase was a matter of far greater importance than the welfare of their subjects.

In the words of the charter by which John disafforested the county of Devon, "the men residing in it, and their heirs shall be altogether disafforested and acquitted, and free for us and our heirs for ever of all things which to forest and foresters appertain, except the two moors above named, to wit, Dartmoor and Exmoor by the aforesaid bounds." It has, however, been doubted whether the county was effectually disafforested by this charter.

In the year 1239 Henry III. granted the forest of Dartmoor, and the manor and castle of Lydford to his brother Richard, Earl of Poictou and Cornwall, consequent upon which Dartmoor was in law no longer a forest, but became a chase, as none but the king can possess the former, unless under a special grant. However, that portion of the old moor lying within the bounds set forth in the Perambulation, has always retained the name of forest, and is never spoken of as a chase. It must not be imagined that the word forest, as applied to Dartmoor, possesses any other signification than that of a tract of land where the beasts of the chase were hunted, and which was placed under the forest laws, and it by no means necessarily implies the presence of thick woods. Such could never have existed upon Dartmoor, although it is probable that there was formerly brushwood, and perhaps small oak trees in the more sheltered combes, among which the beasts might find a lair. There were curious tenures of land around Dartmoor closely connected with hunting, on the "old, wild forest." David of Sciredun* held a virgate of land at that place on condition of his finding two arrows when the King came to hunt in Dartmoor; Walter de Deveneys held the same place (Sciredun) upon the service of finding three arrows; Odo Arch, as also Walter de Bromhall, in the reign of Edward I., held lands in Droscumbe, for a like service, with the addition of a bow and

* Skerraton, in the parish of Dean.

William de Albemarle held the manor of Loston in the same reign on the service of finding two arrows and one loaf of bread.

We have no record setting forth the bounds of the forest referred to in the charter of King John, but we possess copies of a Perambulation made thirty-six years later, namely in 1240, the year following the bestowal of the forest upon Richard, Earl of Cornwall. This was done in order that Richard might get the bounds of his forest or chase duly settled, and the Perambulation was made by twelve knights of the county. It must be understood that the holding of the forest by the earl did not dispossess the commoners of the rights which they had upon it previously to its having been granted to him, for the charter of John expressly states that the men of Devon and their heirs were to have the customs within the regards of those moors which they were wont to have in the time of King Henry I. The Perambulators began their survey of the bounds of the forest at Cosdon, a high hill in the north-east part of the moor. From its summit the view is most extensive and varied. Exmoor is plainly visible, and the Bristol Channel, off Bideford Bay, may also be seen ; while towards the south-east a glimpse of the English Channel is to be obtained. There are many antiquities on and near the hill of Cosdon which are worthy of an extended examination, and the whole neighbourhood is one which may well detain the lover of nature or the investigator of the pre-historic monuments of the moor. Taw Plain should certainly be visited. It is an extensive level stretch at the foot of Cosdon, entirely surrounded by hills, the only openings to it being the narrow gorges where the Taw and a tributary stream enter it at its higher end, and one by which the river named leaves it. Steeperton Tor, at its southern end, is finely placed, and is a bold, striking eminence.

On what particular part of Cosdon the Perambulators set forth on their journey around the ancient forest we cannot now with certainty determine, and indeed the bounds as specified by them vary considerably in many parts of the moor from those generally recognised at the present day. Some of the spots mentioned in this Perambulation can now be scarcely identified, and the boundary line of the duchy does not always agree with that which the commoners of certain of the parishes surrounding the forest consider to be the correct one.

From Cosdon the line which the Perambulators took led them to Little Hound Tor, whence, pursuing a southerly direction, they reached the Teign, and passed onward to King's Oven, which is not very far from the present high road that crosses the moor from Princetown to Moretonhampstead. Thence down the Wellabrook until that stream falls into the East Dart, when the latter became the boundary as far as Dartmeet. The Perambulators then ascended the West Dart to the point where that river receives the waters of the Wobrook, which stream becomes in turn the boundary. Just above a spot now known as Horse Ford the Perambulators left the stream, and proceeding over the hill in due time reached the source of another. This was the Western Wellabrook, and their course lay along it to its confluence with the Avon. The Perambulation says that the line then goes to Ester Whyteburghe (Eastern Whitaburrow), but this, which is a fine cairn, twelve yards high and ninety yards in circumference, is now looked upon as standing some distance without the bounds, and it is probable that Western Whitaburrow was meant. This is also a cairn, but not so large as the former, and on it formerly stood a granite cross, erected to serve as a boundary mark to Brent Moor, which here abuts on the forest. This cross is mentioned in an inquisition which was held on these bounds, dated 1557, at which time Sir William Petre, who owned the manor of Brent, possessed certain rights on the moor.*

From Western Whitaburrow the line proceeds to Red Lake and the Erme, and crossing the Plym runs on to Siward's Cross, and from thence to South Hisworthy, or, as it is now more often called, Look-Out Tor, and so on to North Hisworthy Tor. This is the commanding eminence which overlooks Princetown on the west, and the visitor to that place will do well to follow the example of the old Perambulators and climb to its breezy summit, for he will be be rewarded by a view of such extent and of such varied character as is not often to be obtained. The line proceeds from Hisworthy to Great Mis Tor, a truly magnificent pile of granite rocks, which the sojourner at Princetown should also endeavour to visit. Across the Walkham the Perambulators made their way, and so on to Lynch Tor, and Western Red Lake which they followed to the Tavy, and then proceeding to Rattlebrook foot they ascended that stream, and passing over the ridge descended to Sandy Ford on the West Ockment. Across the heathery sweep that stretches from the summit of High Willes southerly, to a tributary of the stream just named, they pursued their course to the upper waters of the Black-a-vain Brook, which they followed to the East Ockment. Thence over the hill on which is the fine range of tors near Belstone, and down to the Taw, at the foot of the hill of Cosdon, whence they set out.

The tract of country therefore, comprehended by these bounds, and which extends north and south for a distance of seventeen miles, and having an average breadth of about six miles, formed the forest or chase of which the Earl of Cornwall became the possessor.

There is no doubt that this forest yielded some considerable revenue to its owner, derived principally from the charges for the agistment of cattle, and from the tin mines. Mining was at this period carried on to no inconsiderable extent upon the moor, and it has been said that Richard obtained the means to purchase the title of King of the Romans from the stannaries pertaining to the earldom.

In the year 1300 the forest reverted to the crown, after having been held by Henry, the eldest son of Earl Richard, for a short time, and for a period of twenty-eight years by Edmund, Henry's brother. It remained in the hands of the crown during the last seven years of the reign of Edward I., the twenty years of Edward the Second's reign, and the first ten of Edward the Third's, at the end of which period

* I have given a full account of this cross and of its destruction in my work on *The Ancient Crosses of Dartmoor*.

in 1337, the king raised the earldom of Cornwall into a duchy, creating his son Edward, afterwards the Black Prince, the first duke. The forest or chase of Dartmoor was then bestowed upon him, and became an appanage of the duchy, and such it has ever since remained.

The eldest son of the sovereign, the Prince of Wales, is always Duke of Cornwall, until he succeeds to the throne, and the forest is therefore vested in him. In the case of there being no Prince of Wales living, it reverts to the crown until there is one.

When in 1300 the crown became possessed of Dartmoor, it was given into the custody of John de Tresympel, and among the profits arising therefrom, and of which he renders accounts, are the following items: £4 12s. 8d. rent of assize, "as it is contained in the Roll of particulars which he delivered into the Treasury;" 18s. 8d. of increment of rent; 33s. 4d. for the water-mill; 13s. 6d. "de mortuo gabulo;" £4 1s. 8d. "de finibus villarum;" 12d. of the village of W——— ; 13s. 10d. of the fines of 83 folds at 2d. per fold. There are several others of a similar nature, and they amount altogether to £58 10s. 5d., for the year ending Michaelmas 1301.

In 1307 Edward II. conferred Dartmoor upon Piers Gaveston, his favourite, who however held it only for four years, for upon his capture and execution at Warwick, it again fell into the King's hands, and was committed to the custody of Thomas le Ercedekne, constable of Lydford Castle. In 1314 the bailiwick of Dartmoor was placed in the hands of Thomas de Shirigge, and some three years after the chase was granted to Hugh de Audley and his wife, Margaret, who was the niece of the King, to be held during the life of the lady.

In 1319 license was granted by Edward to De Audley and his wife to demise the chase to the Abbot of Tavistock for five years, and in 1327 the King granted the bailiwick and forestership of Dartmoor to Richard Caleware, his butler. Margaret de Audley died in 1342, so that when Edward, the Black Prince, was created Duke of Cornwall it was the reversion of Dartmoor that was granted to him, and it did not fall into his hands until the date named, which was five years later.

There have been Perambulations, at various times, of the bounds of the forest, and though they do not quite agree with those set forth by the Perambulators of 1240, yet they do not differ to any great extent in the main. The return to a writ by which a Perambulation was ordered in the reign of James I. sets out the bounds more fully than that of 1240. This was presented at a Court of Survey, held at Okehampton in 1609, before Sir William Strode, Richard Connocke, auditor of the Duchy of Cornwall, Robert Moore and Robert Paddon. It is very interesting, and in addition to setting forth the bounds of the forest, gives some information respecting the rights of the commoners.

Of the mediæval antiquities of Dartmoor, the old granite crosses are perhaps the most striking. Mention has already been made of Siward's Cross as forming one of the boundary marks of the forest, and we therefore know that it was standing so early as 1240. It is a very fine specimen of these interesting memorials of other days, and is about two-and-a-half miles from Princetown. The visitor may reach it by following the path that leads from the latter place by the side of the Railway Inn, towards South Hisworthy, or Look-Out Tor. A new-take wall, which he must follow will lead him past the Tor for some little distance. At the corner of the new-take, the wall should be left, and the same direction the pedestrian has been pursuing be continued. A boundary bank will then be seen along which the path leads direct to the cross.

Standing over seven feet in height, Siward's, or Nun's Cross as it is now more generally called, is a striking object, and the visitor will scarcely fail to be impressed at finding this symbol of the Christian faith here in the silent moor. It is fixed in a socket-stone, sunk in the ground, and the shaft is broken, this old cross having been thrown down about the year 1846. This was done by two lads, who were out looking for cattle in this part of the moor, and finding that the cross rocked in its socket, pushed it over, when falling across a corner of the stone the shaft broke in two. It did not lie long, however, in a prostrate condition, as all who are interested in the preservation of our Dartmoor antiquities will rejoice to hear. Being again set up, and having the fractured shaft repaired with iron clamps, it was fixed firmly in its socket with wedges.

Siward's Cross is the only one on the moor that bears any inscription. On its eastern face, that is to say, on the side toward the forest, is the word *Siward*, or *Syward*,—it is difficult to determine whether the second letter is an *i* or a *y*,—and on its western face, immediately below a small incised cross, is an inscription which has been read as *Roolande*, but which the writer believes to be *Boclond*, and has elsewhere given his reason for arriving at this conclusion.* The monks of Buckland—anciently Boclond, received the manor of Walkhampton, which extended forestward as far as the cross, from Amicia, Countess of Devon, in the time of Edward I., and it is mentioned on the deed by which she gave that manor, together with others, for the purpose of building and supporting the abbey. In order to mark the boundary of their possessions the monks very probably cut the name of their abbey upon the face of the cross which looked over their lands.

This time-worn stone also served the purpose of marking the direction of the Abbots' Way, an old road that passed over the moor, and of which traces may still be seen in certain spots. It formed a means of communication between the abbeys of Buckland and Tavistock on one side of the moor, and that of Buckfast on the other. The date of the foundation of this latter house was 1137, and it is therefore probable that for a period of some four hundred years this track was constantly travelled over by the monks. There are several other ancient ways on the moor, and they are not the least interesting of the marks which the men of a bygone day have left upon it.

Another cross, standing upon a calvary, formerly existed below Fox Tor, on its northern side, but it unfortunately fell by the vandalism of a farmer, about the year 1812. A tradition states that it marked

* *Ancient Crosses of Dartmoor*, p. 29, *et. seq.*

the last resting-place of one Childe, a hunter, who was there found frozen to death, and who had slain his horse and disembowelled him, in order that, by creeping within the carcase, he might shield himself from the bitter winter blast. Whatever foundation there was for the legend is lost in obscurity, but that it is one which at least possesses the respectability of age is certain, for our old topographer of Devonshire, Tristram Risdon, who wrote his Survey of the county between 1605 and 1630, refers to the story and the cross, which latter he characterizes as one of Dartmoor's "three remarkable things," the other two being Crockern Tor and Wistman's Wood. Childe is stated to have written with his blood his last testament, as follows :

"They fyrste that fyndes and bringes mee to my grave,
The priorie of Plimstoke they shall have !"

The monks of Tavistock are stated to have fulfilled these conditions and so obtained the reward of Childe's lands. As, however there was no Priory of Plymstock, and the manor being possessed by the Abbey of Tavistock at the time of the Domesday Survey, it is certain that there is some confusion here. Prince in his *Worthies of Devon* states that Childe is supposed to have lived in Edward the Third's reign, but he does not give any grounds for this. That the story is a distortion of some Saxon legend seems not unlikely, and the name of the mythic hunter very probably a corruption of the Saxon word Cild, a common appellation. The monks may have acquired the Plymstock lands by means which they considered it were better should not be known, and perhaps invented the story to account for their holding them ; we know they scrupled not to do such things, believing, we may suppose, that the end justified the means, and as long as they could secure wealth for Mother Church it mattered little how they came by it.

There are about thirty crosses on the moor altogether, several of them still maintaining an erect position. Among the principal may be named Huntingdon Cross, marking a boundary of Brent Moor, Roman's Cross on Lee Moor, the Windypost, not far from the road leading from Merivale Bridge to Tavistock, and Bennett's Cross, near the Warren House Inn, on the road from Post Bridge to Moretonhampstead. They are all of them interesting, and carry us back to a time when men were more devout, and found delight at seeing the symbol of their faith planted by the wayside. On the border-land of Dartmoor, crosses are also to be found, few parishes being without one or more of them, though, unfortunately, many have been mutilated.

The remains of old tin workings are also well worthy of examination by the curious investigator of the moor. There is not a valley but has been visited by the streamer, and in many of them the heaps of stones extend for a long distance, showing that a vast amount of labour must have been expended in the washing of the tin ore from the gravels. Many curious erections of the tinners of mediæval times are to be seen near them. These consist of the ruins of small rectangular buildings, constructed all upon one plan, some of them showing signs of having been blowing-houses, that is, houses in which the ore was smelted. In these may sometimes be seen small hollows sunk in granite stones which served as moulds to receive the melted tin; and others of a different shape were probably mortars in which the ore was pounded. Old wheel pits, and the remains of water-courses may also be observed, and many other signs of extensive mining operations.

When the tinners of the counties of Devon and Cornwall formed one body they used to meet for the purpose of framing their laws and transacting the business of the stannaries on Hingeston Down in Cornwall. On separating they still continued to hold Parliaments, the first held by the tinners of Devon, of which we have any account being on the 14th day of September, 1494, at Crockern Tor, on Dartmoor, but it is certain that they had met there long previous to that time. When the two bodies separated we do not know, but that it was as early as 1305 a charter of that date proves, for in it the stannaries and tinners of Cornwall are referred to as distinct from those of Devon.

We know not when the laws which regulated the stannaries were instituted, but we are sure that they are of very remote origin; and also that the stannaries themselves were early looked upon as being the King's demesne. The dues were a source of considerable profit, and very stringent indeed were the laws which enforced their payment, but the tinners on their side were possessed of considerable privileges. No tin was allowed to be removed from the stannary before it had been weighed and stamped, and neither "man or woman, Christian or Jew," was allowed to have any in their possession beyond a fortnight without this being done, neither in or out of the stannary. When the weighing and stamping had been attended to, the tin was to be taken within a period of thirteen weeks to the place appointed for refining it, and the dues were to be paid to the treasurers. It was even then not allowed to be removed out of the counties of Devon and Cornwall without a license from the chief warden of the stannaries, and to prevent this law being evaded, persons were appointed in the various ports of these counties to cause all mariners that landed there to take an oath that they would not convey away in their ships any tin that had not been duly weighed and stamped, and for which a license for its removal had not been granted by the warden.

All tin found in the stannary of Devon was to be weighed, according to the charter of Edward I. in 1305, at Tavistock, Ashburton, or Chagford, each of which is situated close to the borders of the moor. In 1328 Plympton was created a stannary town in the place of Tavistock, but the latter was afterwards restored to its former position, for in the account of the first Parliament on Crockern Tor, in 1494, of which we have already made mention, all the four places are named as stannary towns.

Crockern Tor is near the centre of Dartmoor, and about equidistant from these towns, thus proving a suitable spot for the tinners to meet at, but we can scarcely understand in these days the holding of a Parliament in the open air on the summit of a Tor, exposed to all the inclemencies of the weather. But it long continued to be the place where the hardy stannators met and made their laws, the court consisting of a president, and twenty-four jurors from each of the four towns. A precept dated 1703 from the vice-warden, the Honourable Samuel Rolle, sets forth that Lord Granvill, warden of the Stannaries appointed a Parliament of tinners to assemble on the Tor on the 20th day of September, at eight o'clock in the morning! What would our legislators of the present day say to being summoned to meet on a Dartmoor hill to make laws at such an hour? We fancy such a prospect would cause many of them to pause before seeking the honours of public service.

There were formerly stone seats, a stone table and judge's chair to be seen on the Tor, but these were unfortunately removed towards the close of the last century, and one of Dartmoor's most interesting antiquities destroyed. A large flat stone forming a canopy over a spring in the farm court of Dunnabridge is said to have been brought from Crockern Tor, and if so was probably the table around which the stannators met. The dolmen already referred to as existing immediately within the gate of Dunnabridge Pound has been pointed out as formerly being the judge's chair on the Tor, but this was obviously an error. The Tor is not far from Two Bridges, on the Moreton road, and may be easily reached from Princetown. Indeed, a fine walk may be taken from the latter place, which will enable the visitor to see Risdon's "three remarkable things," and Nun's Cross as well, and which would not extend to more than about twelve miles. The cross should first be visited, then Childe's Tomb under Fox Tor, care being taken in proceeding to the latter to leave Fox Tor Mire on the left. Then, as the West Dart would have to be crossed, the pedestrian should make for Prince Hall Bridge, and passing behind the house proceed by the carriage drive to the Ashburton road. Crockern Tor will then be in sight, and a bee line may be made for it across Muddy Lakes New-take, and after having examined it, a walk of no great length will bring the visitor to Wistman's Wood. The return journey will be by way of Two Bridges, and if the day be fine the walk will be found a most enjoyable one, and it is needless to say, full of interest.

The "lonely Wood of Wistman" is situated on the left bank of the West Dart, about a mile above Two Bridges. The ancient oak trees grow amid a clatter of rocks, and so stunted in their growth are they that many have their boughs resting on the blocks of granite that encumber the ground, and while this confused clatter has been the cause of the dwarfish growth of the oaks of Wistman, it has at the same time aided in their preservation. Had not the young saplings received the shelter which it has afforded, in all probability Wistman's Wood long ere this would have disappeared. To-day it forms one of the curiosities of Dartmoor, and it is to be hoped that it will long flourish amid the gray rocks of its silent valley. It is probable that in other combes on the moor might formerly be seen similar small oak woods, though that tree now only grows in a very few spots upon it. Piles Wood on the Erme, and Black Tor Copse on the West Ockment are both very much like Wistman's Wood, and though

Crockern Tor

Wistman's Wood

Cranmere Pool

The Dewerstone

The Island of Rocks

Ockerry Bridge

Bellaford Tor

Tor Royal, Princetown

The Prison, Princetown

their praises have not been so often sung, yet they possess mucn tnat cannot fail to attract.

In the northern part of Dartmoor is situated Cranmere Pool, well worthy a visit on account of its wild surroundings. The West Ockment, the Tavy, the East Dart and the Taw all take their rise in the morasses which surround it, but it is not actually the source, as sometimes has been stated, of any of the Dartmoor rivers. Although it still retains the name it is a pool no longer, for its bank having been dug through, it is incapable of holding water in any quantity. What little now collects within its basin speedily runs through the broken bank, and goes to augment the waters of the West Ockment. Tradition tells us that the pool was drained dry by one Binjie Gear, who being condemned for some reason, but what the legend does not inform us, to dip out its waters with an oat-sieve, one day found a sheep-skin on the moor, and covering the sieve with it was enabled to empty Cranmere, and no water has ever collected within it since. The pool is situated at an elevation of nearly 1900 feet, and in order to reach it the visitor must pass over some of the roughest ground and through some of the wildest parts of Dartmoor. There is a small heap of stones in it, in which is a tin box, where visitors may deposit their cards, or write their names and date of visit in the note-book provided. It is to be hoped that all those who may thread their way over the bogs to inspect the pool will commit no act of vandalism by removing the cards or autographs they may find there.

Cranmere is mentioned by William of Worcester, who in the year 1478, passed through Okehampton on his journey from Bristol to St. Michael's Mount.

The Dewerstone, below which the waters of the Mew and the Plym unite, is a spot much favoured by visitors, its proximity to a railway station within a few miles of Plymouth, rendering it easy of access. It is near here that the spectre huntsman with his Wish hounds is said to pursue the chase by night, when above the roaring of the wind may be heard the cracking of the whip and the deep baying of the spectral hounds. Carrington, the poet of Dartmoor, has given us some beautiful lines on this charming spot.

One of the most interesting and amusing of the superstitions connected with the moor, is that which formerly obtained regarding the pixies. Now-a-days few, if any, actually believe the stories related of them, but the old people on the moor will nevertheless tell you that faith was placed in them when they were young. The pixies are a race of elves, said to be the souls of unbaptized children, who seem to delight in playing pranks with the farm people, and with the lonely wanderer over the moor. It is, however, generally to be noticed in the tales told of them that they are oftener desirous of helping the farmer than of causing him annoyance, and when the latter has been the case there has generally been some very good cause for it. Even when the traveller has been led astray, or "pixy-led," as it is termed, it would appear that it has been done in order to draw him from their haunts, and not with any desire to work him harm. Sometimes one of these elves has been captured, so the stories tell us, but has almost invariably made its escape quickly afterwards ; the writer in his wanderings over Dartmoor during the past twenty years, has never yet chanced upon one himself, although he has been out upon the moor at all seasons and at all hours of the day and night. Nor, indeed, has he ever yet discovered anybody else who has seen one ; when he does he will not fail to obtain as complete a description of the little sprite as is possible, and make it known to all who may care to inform themselves about it. He does not, however, hold out any hopes of so doing. But he can at any rate record something of what he has learnt from the Dartmoor peasants respecting the doings of the "little people," leaving the reader to believe it or not as he may list.

Not very far from the beautiful glen known as the Island of Rocks, to the westward of High Willes and Yes Tor, in the neigbourhood of Okehampton, a labourer was on one occasion making his way homeward. A net hanging across his shoulder pointed somewhat too plainly to the fact that he had been poaching, but, judging from appearances with ill success. The shades of evening were closing around him, and the faint track he was pursuing amid the heather could scarcely be discerned. The only sound that broke the stillness was the murmuring of the Ockment as it sped on over its pebbly bed, and the soft sighing of the wind as it gently waved the tall ferns that grew plentifully on the slopes around. Suddenly the peasant stopped, his eyes rivetted on something a short distance ahead of him. Then, moving cautiously forward, he saw that it was a hare among the heather that had attracted his attention, and with a sudden bound he snatched up the little animal and thrust it quickly into a bag that he was carrying, and went upon his way, delighted at his unexpected bit of luck. Soon the stunted oaks and ancient hollies of Okehampton Park were reached, and the peasant grasped his bag tightly and hurried on as fast as he could, for in the deepening gloom of the evening he knew not what of "wishtness" there might be ready to pounce out upon him from behind those old trees. Just as he reached a part more gloomy than any he had yet passed a shrill voice called out, at some short distance from him, "Jack How ! Jack How !" Instantly the hare began to struggle and crying out, "Ho ! ho ! there's my daddy," managed somehow to make his escape from the bag, ere the astonished peasant could comprehend what had occurred. All he could understand from the mysterious circumstance was that he had snatched up a pixy that had for the time assumed the form of a hare.

Another story is related of the capture of a pixy by an old dame at the Ockerry Bridge, between Princetown and Two Bridges. Seeing the little fellow jumping and capering on the path before her, she seized upon him at a moment when he seemed to be off his guard, and placed him in her basket for safety. The little elf commenced to talk rapidly in a language she could not understand, and becoming tired, we may suppose, of doing all the talking and receiving no replies, at length ceased. When the dame peeped into her basket to ascertain whether her little prisoner was safe, she found he had flown. As she had securely fastened the cover of the basket she could only conjecture that he had contrived to squeeze himself through the wicker-work; at all events he was gone, and the hope of taking home such a prize was not to be realized.

On one occasion, a nurse was summoned by an old fellow to attend upon his wife, who was about to add to the population of the moorland district. When the little stranger arrived, the good woman was handed some ointment with which she was told to anoint its eyes. She did so, and at the same time, in order to see what effect it would produce, she touched one of her own eyes with it. Instantly she saw that she had been introduced into a pixy family, but said nothing to lead the father or mother to imagine she had made the discovery. A short while after, being at a market on the borders of the moor, she saw the old pixy, bustling about among the crowd of people, and accosted him. "Holloa," said the old fellow, "Can you see me?" "See you?" replied the woman, "Why of course I can." "With which eye do you see me?" demanded the pixy. "With the right," answered the dame. Without a moment's warning, the elf raised his hand and struck her a violent blow on the organ she had named, and she was ever after blind in it. This was the penalty she had to pay for daring to use the fairy ointment, which had enabled her to see what had been invisible to others.

Nor, it seems, must the pixy revels be intruded upon. Tom White, of Post Bridge, many years ago, found this out to his cost. Tom was greatly attached to a buxom dairymaid at Huccaby Farm, and nightly made a pilgrimage of nearly five miles, over the moor, to visit her, and bask for a few short hours in the sunshine of her smiles. There could be no mistaking the ardour of his passion, for, unless he had been very much in love, he would scarcely have undertaken a walk of ten miles every night. And so others, who had looked with longing eyes upon the damsel, thought, and considering it hopeless to contend with such a doughty rival, left the field clear for Tom. One night he had remained rather later than usual, for which, all who have had any experience in similar matters, will be ready to excuse him, and actually saw signs of approaching dawn before he had got far upon his homeward way. Walking rapidly on, he soon gained the slopes of Bellaford Tor, and shortly before reaching the pile of hoary rocks, fancied he heard voices. However, he was too anxious to reach home to trouble much about the sounds, and thinking he might very likely have been mistaken, he pushed on. As he passed the Tor, they again struck upon his ear, and he found there was no doubt about the matter now. Merry voices were to be heard plainly enough, and Tom recognized at once that he was near a party of pixies. Stepping from behind a rock, he came upon them, and the sight filled him with wonder. A crowd of little creatures were dancing merrily in a ring, and shouting with glee, while many were also perched upon the granite rocks scattered around. His first impulse was to fly, and he turned, hoping to do so unperceived. But the pixy eyes were sharp, and ere Tom White could move a step, he found himself surrounded by the elves, who danced furiously in a circle about him, and to his amazement, he felt compelled to join them, and was soon dancing frantically, and whirling around with them, but yet, so rapidly did they move, being unable to keep pace with the agile sprites. Tom implored them to stop, but they only laughed at him, and though his legs were beginning to tire, and he would have given anything to have been able to cease dancing, he was utterly unable to do so, but was constrained to continue until the sun peeped up beyond the eastern hills, when he instantly dropped to the ground, and the pixies vanished.

The sequel is a sad one. The pixies seem to have danced all Tom's pluck out of him, for he never visited the damsel of Huccaby any more. While he could return to his home at night, filled with the bliss of "love's young dream," in a steady and sensible manner, he was equal to any amount of toil for the sake of his lady-love, but when it came to being compelled to dance hornpipes on Bellaford Tor, in the middle of the night, Tom felt his fate was being cut out for him a little too roughly, and frankly stated such, saying, "he did'n main to go courtin' again."

And the pixies are equally jealous of having their power doubted, as they are of being intruded upon at their revels. Poor Nanny Norrish, a washer-woman, and better half of a humble pedagogue, who once resided at Dunstone Cottage, near the church-town of Widecombe, was very sceptical about what they were stated to be able to do, and always treated the narration of their pranks by others, with the greatest contempt. But one night Nanny received a fright, and never after did she laugh at the pixies. Having finished her day's work at Dockwell, in Widecombe parish, she set out for her home, being warned by the people to beware of the little sprites, and see that she did not get pixy-led. But she would scarcely listen to what was said, and loudly expressed her belief that she should never meet with one. In this, however, she was mistaken, for when she was some distance on her road, she suddenly found it completely blocked by pixies, who perched upon one another's heads, formed a pyramid of great height, and utterly prevented her from passing. She was frightened in no small degree, and repented of ever having spoken in dispraise of the elfin tribe, and how she reached her home, eventually, we know not, but the pixies fully revenged themselves by giving her a good fright, and leaving her no room to be sceptical of their power in the future.

Many tales are related of moorland farmers having their corn threshed for them by the pixies, and in cases where they have not been interfered with, they have been the means of conferring great benefit upon those they have helped, but immediately their actions have been pryed into, they have ceased to do any more good. Lazy maidservants are punished by them, their toes being pinched by the elves if they rise not betimes from their beds. Milk has been turned sour by their agency, where careless dairymaids have needed some sharp lesson to cause them to be attentive to their work, and candles have been blown out (especially where there has been *a strong draught*), to vex the idle domestics. The traveller, too, has often been pixy-led, and must be careful under such circumstances not to forget the charm for this, otherwise, how long he may have to wander aimlessly upon the moor, it is impossible to say. Should he find himself in such an unfortunate predicament, he must not fail to turn one of his garments inside out, and wear it; this will soon set matters straight.*

The modern history of Dartmoor may be said to commence with the building of Tor Royal, in 1798, by Sir Thomas Tyrwhitt, who, however, began operations on the moor, thirteen years previously. He was very sanguine that much might be done on Dartmoor, in the way of cultivation, but results have not justified his expectations. Many besides Sir Thomas have formed the same idea, expressing a belief that what they are pleased to call the waste land of Dartmoor, might be profitably cultivated. Not a few have given practical proof of their faith, and as a result a good deal of money has been lost on the moor. As old Dartmoor is jocularly supposed to say to all who think that they can metamorphose him: "If thee scratch my back, thee shalt smart for't," and so many have found out, and have had to pay dearly for their whistle. Besides, Dartmoor cannot be said to be waste land. It is put to its best economical use as a pasturage for cattle, sheep, and ponies, being stocked with many thousands yearly.

A few years after Sir Thomas Tyrwhitt had built Tor Royal, he conceived the idea that a site under North Hisworthy Tor, and not far from his newly-formed estate, would be a suitable one on which to erect a prison, where the war captives, who then crowded the prisons at Plymouth, might be located. The plan was approved of by the Government, and in 1806, Sir Thomas laid the first stone of the buildings, and in 1808 they were opened. As many as ten thousand men, French and Americans, were confined in them at one time, and this necessitating a large staff of officials, and the location of soldiers as a guard, many houses were built close by, and so Princetown came to be formed. One can scarcely approve the judgment of Sir Thomas and the men of his day, in fixing upon such a spot on which to build a prison of war. There seems to be no reason why men should be punished for fighting for their country. Detained they must, of course, be, if they fall into the enemy's hands, but there is a difference between that and placing them in a dreary looking prison, on a bleak part of the moor, fourteen hundred feet above the sea.

However, when Napoleon was routed at Waterloo, and the war was shortly after brought to a close, the prisons were no longer needed, and Princetown became partially deserted. The huge buildings were for a time used for a manufacturing purpose, but with no success, and in 1850 were fitted up as a convict depôt. This, the old war prison, has ever since continued to be, many very extensive alterations and additions having, from time to time, been made to it.

The Dartmoor tram-road was also the proposal of Sir Thomas Tyrwhitt, and was first opened in 1823. In his statement which he

* The writer would mention his *Tales of the Dartmoor Pixies*, as containing a full account of the reputed antics of this elfin race.

laid before the Plymouth Chamber of Commerce in 1818 he pointed out the great benefits likely to accrue from its construction, showing what a number of commodities would be conveyed over it. These hopes were only faintly realised. The tram-road was eventually used for bringing granite from the Foggin Tor quarries to the Laira Bridge above Cattewater, and this traffic was continued until the formation of the Princetown Railway, which runs very nearly on the line of route taken by Sir Thomas's old tram-way.

Princetown forms a capital centre for the tourist, many most interesting spots on the moor being within easy reach of it, and good fishing is to be obtained without going very far for it. Other good points from which to make moorland explorations are Okehampton, Chagford, and Brent. The former affords the best starting-point for Yes Tor, and High Willes, the latter being the highest hill upon the moor, and in fact in the whole of the South of England. It attains an elevation of two thousand and thirty-nine feet, a few feet higher than that of Yes Tor, which previous to the last Ordnance Survey was generally considered the more lofty of the two, though this was sometimes disputed by the moor-men, who are now proved to have been correct. In another place * the writer has given a list of the tors and hills of Dartmoor, with the heights of the principal ones, and so numerous are they that the Tors alone number over a hundred and fifty. Chagford, one of the four stannary towns, has much around it to attract the visitor, a ramble down the noted gorge of Fingle affording much delight to the lover of wild scenery, and the rude stone remains on Shuffle Down, and the dolmen at Drewsteignton, providing ample food for the speculative antiquary. From Brent, the south quarter of the forest may easily be reached, and on the moors which abut upon this, numerous remains of pre-historic times are to be seen. The romantic valley of Dean Burn is within easy walking distance, and Shipley Bridge, and Zeal Pool and Cascades are even nearer. A climb to the summit of Three Barrows will open up to the tourist a most magnificent panorama, the whole of the South Hams, and the South Devon coast lying as it were, at his feet.

To those who are as yet strangers to Dartmoor, the writer would say, visit it as speedily as possible, for there await you attractions you little think of. To those who are acquainted with it, he would offer his congratulations that they have not neglected a spot of so much interest, and at the same time, would express a hope that they may live long to enjoy many a ramble over its breezy heights, drinking in the draughts of pure, invigorating air, and experiencing that feeling of freedom with which this ancient land never fails to inspire the wanderer.

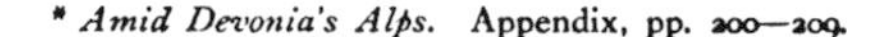

* *Amid Devonia's Alps.* Appendix, pp. 200—209.

INDEX